The birds presented here are in scale to each other.

Sometimes it's more about the journey
than the destination.
To Therese and Jodell,
thank you for your encouragement and inspiration.

Printed and bound in November 2025 at C&C Offset, Shenzhen, China.
www.holidayhouse.com
First Edition
1 3 5 7 9 10 8 6 4 2
ISBN: 978-0-8234-6255-1 (hardcover)

Library of Congress Cataloging-in-Publication Data is available.

EU Authorized Representative: HackettFlynn Ltd, 36 Cloch Choirneal, Balrothery, Co. Dublin, K32 C942, Ireland. EU@walkerpublishinggroup.com

Trumpeter Swan

Light as a Feather

Fifteen Phenomenal North American Birds

Will Hillenbrand

Holiday House New York

Northern Cardinal

Measurements (Both Sexes)
Length: 8.3–9.1 in. (21–23 cm)
Weight: 1.5–1.7 oz. (42–48 g)
Wingspan: 9.8–12.2 in. (25–31 cm)

To find Northern Cardinals, search in areas where people live, such as backyards, parks, and wooded areas. These birds prefer to build their nests in dense bushes and vines. They are found throughout the eastern and southwestern United States, as well as in Mexico and Belize.

FEATHER WEIGHT

Why are feathers so light?

When we want to describe something as light or easy, we often say it is "light as a feather." This is because feathers look and feel airy and delicate to us. Feathers make up only a tiny fraction of a bird's body weight, usually around 5 to 10 percent depending on the species. Yet they are crucial to birds. Feathers insulate them from heat and cold. Birds can fly efficiently and maneuver through the air as well as balance and float on water because of their plumes. Feathers are made of a lightweight protein called keratin, also found in hair, nails, and scales.

Northern Cardinals can sometimes lose all the feathers on their head in a short amount of time. It takes a while for the new feathers to grow in.

During this time, you may see their dark gray to black bald head.

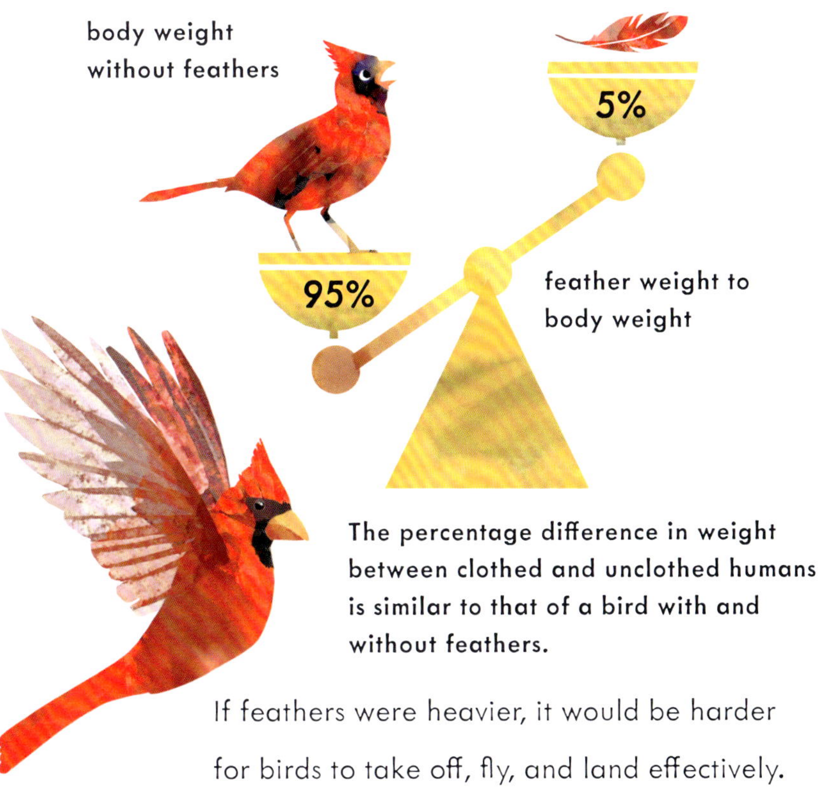

The percentage difference in weight between clothed and unclothed humans is similar to that of a bird with and without feathers.

If feathers were heavier, it would be harder for birds to take off, fly, and land effectively.

Feather Renewal: The fascinating molt cycle of birds

A bird's feathers can show its age, its sex, or the time of year. After the spring and summer breeding seasons, birds shed damaged feathers and grow new ones. This is called molting. The new feathers are sometimes different depending on a bird's age and sex or the season. Although various birds molt differently, if a bird loses a feather, a new one will immediately begin to grow in its place.

Pileated Woodpecker

Measurements (Both Sexes)
Length: 15.8–19.3 in. (40–49 cm)
Weight: 8.8–12.3 oz. (250–350 g)
Wingspan: 26.0–29.5 in. (66–75 cm)

These woodpeckers are commonly found in mature or mixed deciduous-coniferous woodlands, as well as suburban areas with large trees and patches of woodland. Although their populations have steadily increased over time, they, like all birds, are threatened by climate change.

NATURE'S DRUMMERS

WHY DO WOODPECKERS DRUM?

In the spring, a male Pileated Woodpecker drums to tell other Pileated Woodpeckers to stay away from his territory and to advertise for a mate. The sound echoes throughout the forest. But if you listen closely, you might hear the sound of the woodpecker's drumming and even see one nearby.

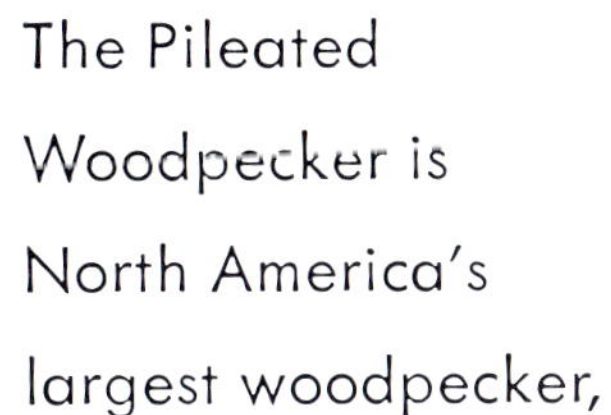

The Pileated Woodpecker is North America's largest woodpecker, and its look is unmistakable. It is a large black bird with white on each side of its neck and a red crest on its head. Pileated Woodpeckers make large holes that other birds like bluebirds, owls, swifts, ducks, martins, and other kinds of woodpeckers can use as homes. It's astonishing how the Pileated Woodpecker helps out other birds!

THEIR TONGUES ARE AMAZING.

A Pileated Woodpecker's skull is designed to absorb and diffuse the pounding from the drumming. Its tongue acts as a shock absorber. It wraps around the skull and cushions the brain from forceful vibrations. The woodpecker's incredibly strong neck muscles help stabilize its head during rapid pecking. Also, the bones in the woodpecker's skull are separated by a spongy bone material, which acts as a natural shock absorber. These unique features let Pileated Woodpeckers drum on trees without getting hurt.

A Pileated Woodpecker has two toes pointing forward and two toes pointing backward that help it hold onto a tree tightly so it can peck harder.

They use their stiff tails for leverage, holding the body away from the tree.

Roseate Spoonbill

Measurements (Both Sexes)

Length: 27.9–33.9 in. (71–86 cm)

Weight: 42.3–63.5 oz. (1,200–1,800 g)

Wingspan:

47.2–51.2 in. (120–130 cm)

Fortunately for Roseate Spoonbills, much of their nesting habitat in Florida occurs in protected areas, including Everglades National Park and national wildlife refuges. However, rising sea levels are forcing them to find new places to forage.

BIRDS WITH BUILT-IN SPOONS

WHY DO BIRDS HAVE DIFFERENT BILL SHAPES?

Bird bills come in many shapes and sizes. Evolution has produced a variety of bill types that allow birds to eat different foods. For birds like the Roseate Spoonbill, their bill shape helps them to forage for food efficiently in their aquatic habitats.

Spoonbills have elongated, spatula-shaped bills that are flattened and widened at the tip, resembling spoons. As they wade through shallow waters, they use their bills to sweep from side to side, scooping up small aquatic invertebrates, fish, and other prey.

These unusual bills demonstrate nature's creativity in adapting animals to various ecological niches and feeding methods. Finches have cone-shaped beaks for cracking seeds. Hummingbirds have long tubular bills for sipping nectar from flowers. Hawks and owls have sharp hooked beaks for holding and tearing apart their prey. Scientists study these adaptations to understand how they contribute to the evolution of bird species.

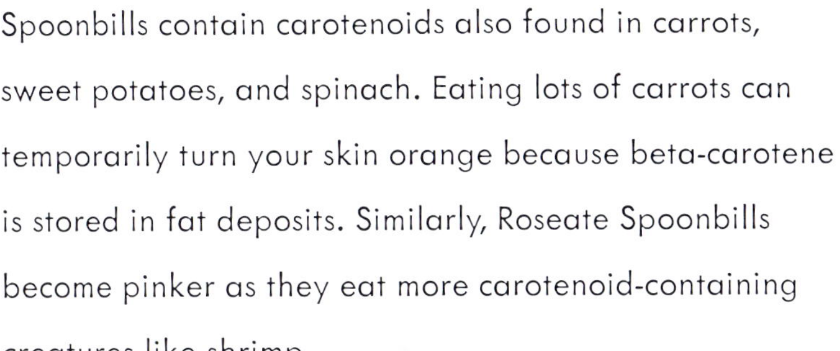

The feathers of Roseate Spoonbills contain carotenoids also found in carrots, sweet potatoes, and spinach. Eating lots of carrots can temporarily turn your skin orange because beta-carotene is stored in fat deposits. Similarly, Roseate Spoonbills become pinker as they eat more carotenoid-containing creatures like shrimp.

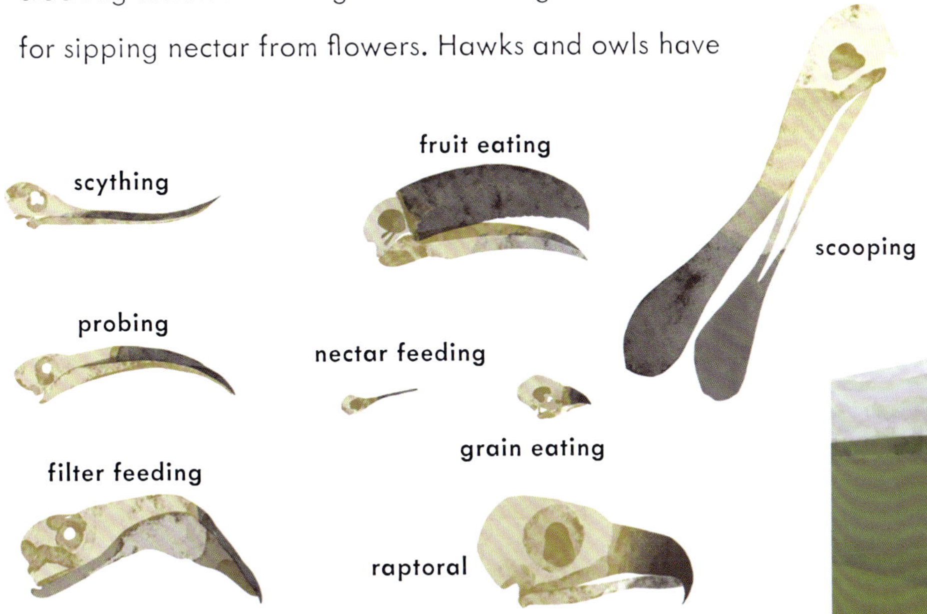

scything

fruit eating

scooping

probing

nectar feeding

grain eating

filter feeding

raptoral

Purple Martin

Measurements (Both Sexes)
Length: 7.5–7.9 in. (19–20 cm)
Weight: 1.6–2.1 oz. (45–60 g)
Wingspan:
15.3–16.1 in.
(39–41 cm)

Purple Martins forage over towns, cities, parks, open fields, dunes, streams, wet meadows, beaver ponds, and other open areas. In the winter, they migrate to South America in the Southern Hemisphere, where the weather will be warm and insects will be thriving. When they return, they look again for abundant populations of insects that appear in the spring and summer. But as climate change affects the seasons, causing spring to come earlier, this could cause Purple Martins to miss the peak population of their prey.

PILOTS OF THE PURPLE TWILIGHT

WHY ARE PURPLE MARTINS SUCH DARING FLYERS?

At twilight, you may witness Purple Martins searching for flying insects. This is because flying insects are more active during this transitional period, which is sometimes called purple twilight. As flying insect eaters, Purple Martins rely on their agility and keen eyesight to capture their prey in midair. The Purple Martin is a type of swallow that is native to North America. Much of their activity is driven by where and when they can find insects.

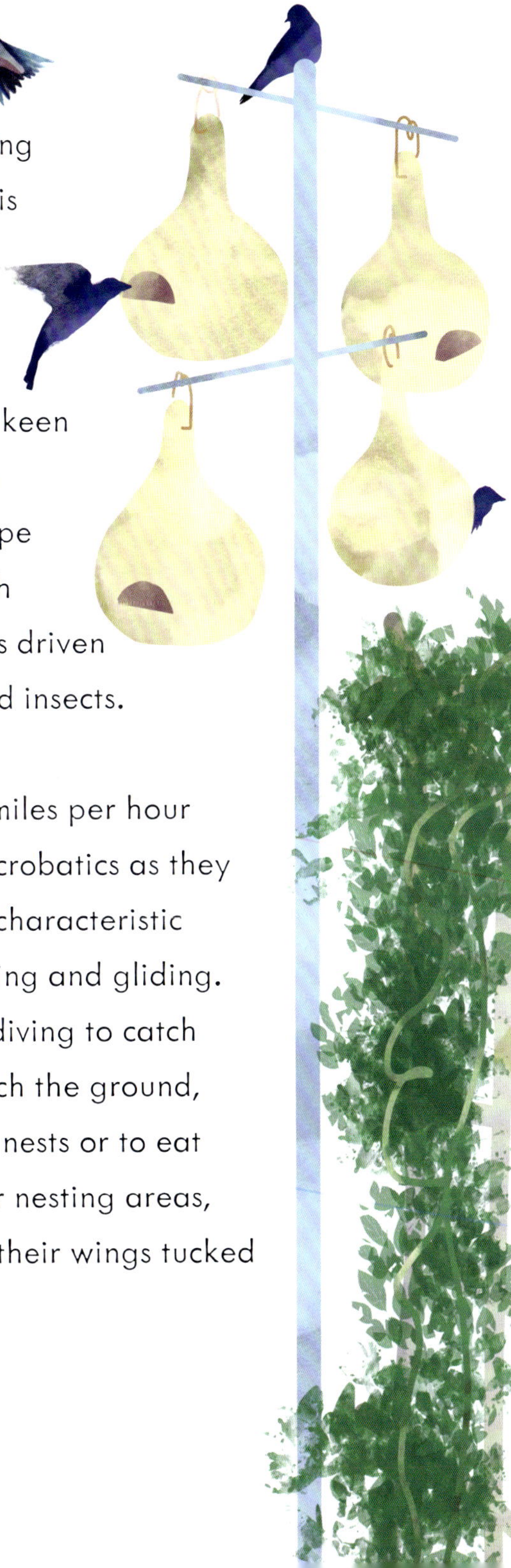

Purple Martins can fly up to 50 miles per hour and are known for their crazy acrobatics as they pursue their prey. They have a characteristic flight pattern mix of rapid flapping and gliding. These birds fly in circles before diving to catch their prey. They hardly ever touch the ground, except to pick up items for their nests or to eat insects. When approaching their nesting areas, they dive with great speed and their wings tucked in, resembling Superman.

What would happen if a fighter pilot tried to perform a sharp turn like a Purple Martin? The human body cannot safely endure such extreme gravitational forces. The maneuver could lead to a potentially fatal loss of control. So it's crucial for pilots to always maintain safe speeds and proper maneuverability even in a dogfight.

A symbiotic relationship between Purple Martins and humans began centuries ago. Before North America was colonized, the Choctaw and Chickasaw people would hang gourds for the birds to nest in, hoping to attract them to help keep insects away from their crops. Today, eastern Purple Martin colonies are almost 100 percent dependent on human-supplied housing. However, western populations still nest in natural cavities such as tree snags or abandoned woodpecker holes.

Eastern Bluebird

Measurements (Both Sexes)

Length: 6.3–8.3 in. (16–21 cm)

Weight: 1.0–1.1 oz. (28–32 g)

Wingspan: 9.8–12.6 in. (25–32 cm)

Uncommon, usually seen in small groups of five to ten. Can be found from Maine to Florida and from the East Coast to the Midwest.

Member of the thrush family. Prefers open, grassy spaces with scattered trees; golf courses; and parks. Nests in tree cavities.

THE BLUEST BIRDS

What makes bluebirds so blue?

Henry David Thoreau wrote that "The bluebird carries the sky on his back." However, it is the structure of their feathers that makes them appear blue. Air pockets and pigment crystals in each feather scatter blue light and absorb other colors. The feather's structure gathers the blue light and directs it outward, creating a beautiful blue color that amazes those who see it.

Only blue escapes; the feather captures all other colors. Our eyes see solely blue on this bird.

Placing a bluebird house at eye level makes it easy to check. However, if cats or other predators are problems, you should hang nest boxes at least six to eight feet from the ground.

In 1960, a man named Dick Peterson noticed that there were fewer bluebirds around. He saw that the places where bluebirds like to live were disappearing. So he decided to make special homes for them called nesting boxes. These boxes were cozy and had a slanted roof to keep away animals that might harm the bluebirds.

The song of an Eastern Bluebird is a soft whistle. This is one of the birds we hear early in spring. Some folks believe they are a sign of joy and hope. Eastern Bluebirds prefer to build their nests in empty cavities, like abandoned woodpecker holes. The female lays one egg a day until she has four to five eggs, but they all hatch on the same day. This is because the mother will only start incubating once all the eggs are laid.

Peterson's idea helped more Eastern Bluebirds come back. He even joined forces with the Audubon Society in Minneapolis to start the Bluebird Recovery Program. They checked the nesting boxes weekly to keep the birds safe and healthy. These checks helped the baby birds grow up strong and happy.

Blue Jay

Measurements (Both Sexes)

Length: 9.8–11.8 in. (25–30 cm)

Weight: 2.5–3.5 oz. (70–100 g)

Wingspan: 13.4–16.9 in. (34–43 cm)

Blue Jays are common, but their populations have declined. Studies have shown that younger Blue Jays are more likely to migrate than older ones.

FLASHY FLYERS

Why do Blue Jays hide acorns?

The Blue Jays' habit of storing food for later not only ensures a consistent supply of food but also highlights their intelligence. They use spatial memory and problem-solving skills to remember the location of their hidden, stored food as needed. Their adaptability and foresight help make them a successful species.

Blue Jays can carry up to five acorns at once.

The migratory patterns of Blue Jays are not consistent. This is one of the more interesting facts about them. Only some populations migrate south during the winter. Others generally stay in their breeding grounds all year.

Blue Jays' habit of storing acorns for the future gives them little incentive to travel for food. They are very adept at recognizing good-quality acorns and can fly with up to five of them at once. It has been found that a Blue Jay may store anywhere between 3,000 and 5,000 acorns during a single autumn. This behavior also helps disperse the acorns so that new oak trees can grow.

Now you see me.

Aposematism is a type of defense that is opposite to camouflage. Some animals, such as Blue Jays, exhibit bright colors to warn predators that they are not easy targets. The flash of blue and white creates a striking color pattern that is believed to protect them from harm. When a Blue Jay feels threatened, it may raise its crest, extend its wings, and produce loud vocalizations to surprise and intimidate the predator. This behavior is meant to make the predator pause or rethink its attack, giving the Blue Jay a chance to escape.

Blue Jays enjoy sunbathing by lying on the ground and spreading their wings. There are a couple of reasons why they do this. Blue Jays benefit from sunlight when they clean their feathers, as the warmth and light can help loosen dirt, bugs, and other unwanted particles that may be stuck to them. The sun's rays also help Blue Jays produce vitamin D, which keeps their bones strong and healthy. Therefore, by soaking up the sun, Blue Jays receive a Vitamin D boost, much like people.

Blue Jay sunning

Sandhill Crane

Measurements (Both Sexes)
Length: 47.2 in. (120 cm)
Weight: 119.9–172.8 oz. (3,400–4,900 g)
Wingspan: 78.7 in. (200 cm)

Rare from the East Coast to the Midwest. Summer in Canada and Oregon, Montana, and Idaho. Migrate to upper and lower Midwest. Summer in Texas and eastern Mexico.

During migration and winter, Sandhill Cranes forage in large flocks on open grassland and in grain fields. They roost at night in shallow water and nest in wet bogs and marshes.

DYNAMIC DANCERS

WHY DO SCIENTISTS PUT BANDS ON BIRDS?

Bird banding is used to study Sandhill Cranes. Researchers gather data on their migration patterns, breeding territories, and changes in population by attaching uniquely numbered bands to each bird. This information helps scientists understand how to protect Sandhill Crane populations that have been declining in some areas due to habitat loss and hunting. Additionally, bird banding has helped to engage the public in Sandhill Crane conservation efforts, allowing citizens and nature enthusiasts to participate in hands-on research and learn about the biology of this magnificent bird. There is strength in numbers as bands give us a more comprehensive picture of how cranes fit into our world.

Is it true that birds have a knee that bends backward? In fact, what appears to be a knee is actually a bird's long ankle. The bird's knee is often hidden by its body and feathers. Additionally, the bone that connects to its hip is proportionally shorter compared to ours.

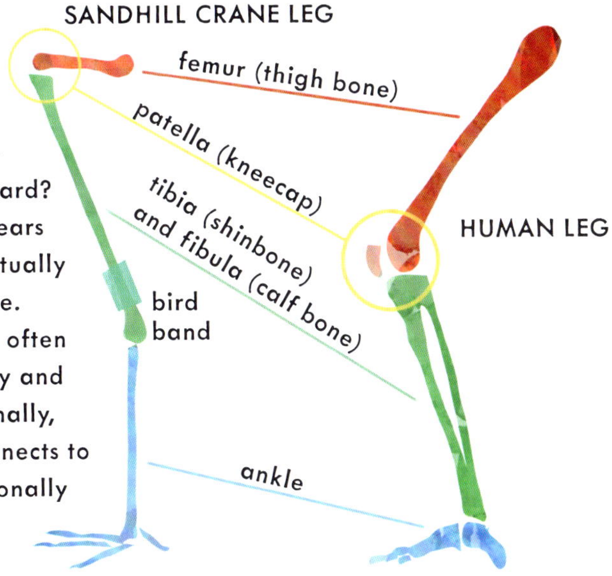

SANDHILL CRANE LEG

HUMAN LEG

femur (thigh bone)

patella (kneecap)

tibia (shinbone) and fibula (calf bone)

bird band

ankle

LEG BONE IS CONNECTED TO THE KNEE BONE

Professional bird banding involves safely capturing birds, handling them carefully, attaching bands with recorded information, and releasing them back into their natural habitats.

Banding is a harmless process that does not hurt the bird. Typically, a band is placed on the bird's leg, specifically on the ankle. In the case of a Sandhill Crane, the band is usually placed above the ankle for better visibility from a distance.

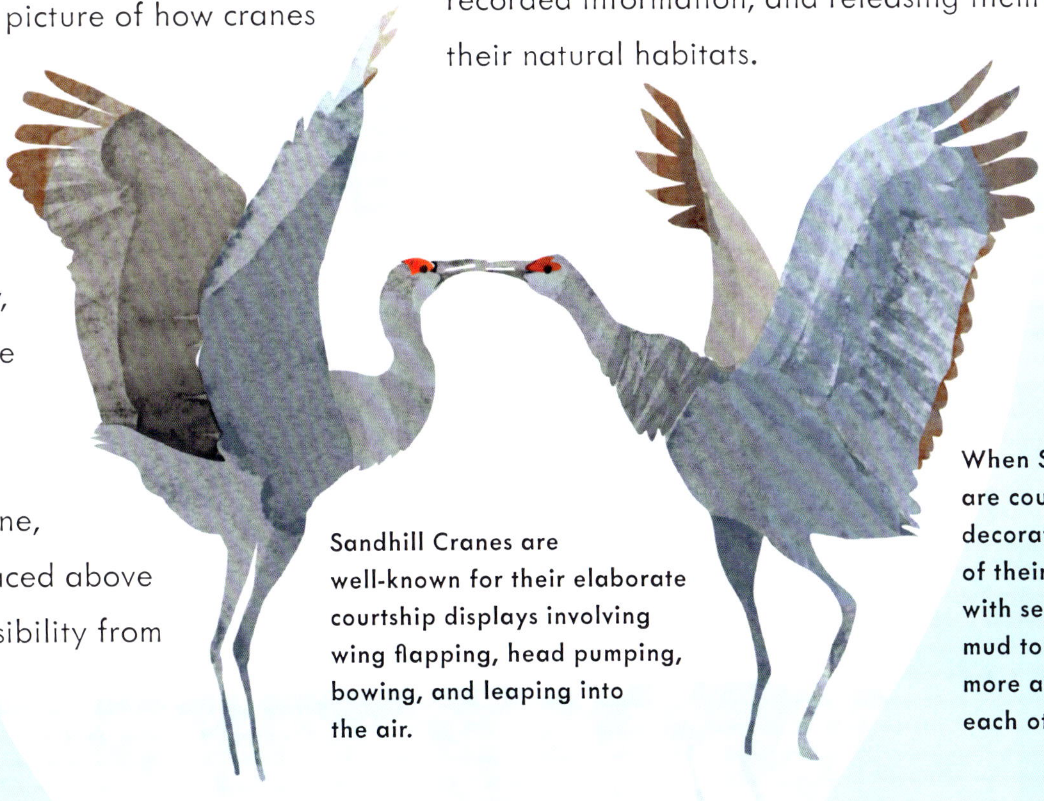

Sandhill Cranes are well-known for their elaborate courtship displays involving wing flapping, head pumping, bowing, and leaping into the air.

When Sandhill Cranes are courting, they decorate the edges of their feathers with sepia-colored mud to make them more attractive to each other.

American Goldfinch

Measurements (Both Sexes)

Length: 4.3–5.1 in.
(11–13 cm)

Weight: 0.4–0.7 oz.
(11–20 g)

Wingspan:
7.5–8.7 in.
(19–22 cm)

American Goldfinches are common, but their numbers have decreased.

GOLDEN GLIDERS

Why do some birds change color seasonally?

The American Goldfinch's colors change dramatically with the seasons. Mature males go though the most drastic change.

The American Goldfinch molts twice a year. The first time is in the spring when the males get their bright yellow and black feathers. These feathers help male goldfinches attract mates during breeding season. The second molt happens at the end of summer when darker gray-green feathers grow in. The duller winter plumage helps the bird hide from predators.

With the second molt, the birds also grow an undercoat of soft feathers. This undercoat helps to keep the small birds warm in cold temperatures. During the winter, they may burrow underneath the snow. However, some American Goldfinches migrate south for the winter and then, in the spring, they begin migrating north.

Goldfinches weave their nests so tight they can temporarily hold water. To keep the nest secure in a tree, they use spiderwebs! They attach the nest to twigs and small branches with the webbing. The nests are small, typically only about 3 inches around and 2 to 4.5 inches high.

Baltimore Oriole

Measurements (Both Sexes)
Length: 6.7–7.5 in. (17–19 cm)
Weight: 1.1–1.4 oz. (30–40 g)
Wingspan: 9.1–11.8 in. (23–30 cm)

Baltimore Orioles are vulnerable to deforestation and habitat loss in many different countries, and their conservation requires international cooperation.

NIFTY NESTERS

How do Baltimore orioles build such Incredible nests?

Baltimore Orioles got their name from the bold orange-and-black plumage matching the colors of the Baltimore family's heraldic crest.

Knot your average nest

The Baltimore Oriole nest is an ideal combination of form and function. Orioles create a hanging basket using plant fibers, grasses, vines, and tree bark, and they even incorporate string or yarn if available, giving the nest a knitted appearance. They secure the nest between small twigs of a branch, anywhere from 6 to 45 feet in the air. It can take up to twelve days for a Baltimore Oriole to weave its nest. One Baltimore Oriole was observed spending 40 hours building a nest with about 10,000 stitches. She tied thousands of knots, all with her beak! By hanging the nest far out on the tips of branches, the birds protect their nestlings from snakes and other predators.

The female builds the nest with little or no help from its mate.

Baltimore Orioles are known for their annual fall migration. They embark on a remarkable journey from their breeding grounds in the eastern United States and fly to their wintering grounds in Mexico, Central America, and some parts of South America. On average, they travel a distance of around 1,500 to 2,000 miles (2,400 to 3,200 kilometers) during their fall migration.

If you put this out, they will come.

Leave out a few orange slices, sweet fruits, or a dollop of grape jelly.

American Kestrel

Measurements (Both Sexes)
Length: 8.7–12.2 in. (22–31 cm)
Weight: 2.8–5.8 oz. (80–165 g)
Wingspan: 20.1–24.0 in. (51–61 cm)

Uncommon in many open habitats from meadows to brushy fields; often seen on roadside wires or fenceposts all over the continental United States.

Hunts mainly for insects and small mammals by hovering and dropping straight down. Habitually bobs its tail when perched.

American Kestrel populations have been declining for decades, and now they are vulnerable to climate change. Studies have shown that when American Kestrels lay their eggs before spring begins, the eggs are more likely to hatch. However, with spring now coming earlier, American Kestrels will need to learn to lay their eggs earlier to survive.

KEEN-EYED HUNTERS

What do you do if you find an injured bird?

Heavy spring rain with strong winds can dislodge baby birds from their nests. If you find a fallen baby bird, handle it with care. First, check if its parents are still around and caring for it. If they are, and the bird seems unharmed, it's best to leave it. If the bird seems injured or the parents are not around, remember you're not alone. Seek professional help. Contact a local wildlife rehabilitation center or a vet, as these experts can provide appropriate care and ensure the bird's safe return to the wild. In Stark County, Ohio, there was a family who found a young American Kestrel that was hurt. They asked a park ranger for help, but the bird's eye injury meant it couldn't go back into the wild. Now, the bird lives at a wildlife rescue center, and the family can visit it there.

To survive in the wild, falcons like the American Kestrel need perfect binocular vision to find and hunt for prey.

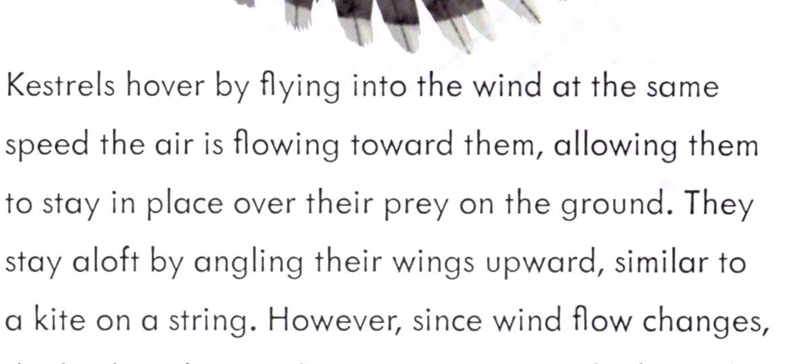

Kestrels hover by flying into the wind at the same speed the air is flowing toward them, allowing them to stay in place over their prey on the ground. They stay aloft by angling their wings upward, similar to a kite on a string. However, since wind flow changes, the birds make rapid movements to steady themselves.

Birds of prey, such as the American Kestrel, rely heavily on their vision. This extraordinary vision is key to their hunting success. As American Kestrels hunt for voles, their favorite food, they can see the voles' scent trails. The urine in the trails reflects the sun's ultraviolet light.

The length of 27 football fields is approximately 1.86 miles. Birds of prey, on average, have exceptional long-range vision. We might see an animal across the length of a football field, but a bird of prey can see it across the length of 27 football fields.

A bird of prey can see a rabbit across over 27 football fields, while we can see it across just one.

Brown Pelican

Measurements (Both Sexes)
Length: 39.4–53.9 in. (100–137 cm)
Weight: 70.5–176.4 oz. (2,000–5,000 g)
Wingspan: 78.7 in. (200 cm)

Found along coasts and in bays and estuaries along the American Pacific coast from western Canada to northern Peru and the American Atlantic coast from the northern United States to northern Brazil.

Life span: 15 to 25 years. However, the oldest known Brown Pelican lived 43 years.

PREHISTORIC PREDATORS

WHY DO PELICANS HAVE POUCHES?

We often associate certain birds with specific locations because they thrive in that area. For example, when traveling to a bay, you might see Brown Pelicans flying overhead or diving into the water to catch fish. The sight of these birds creates a connection in our minds between the Brown Pelican and the bay, making it a recognizable symbol of that particular place.

Brown Pelicans are the only species to dive into the water from 65 feet (19 meters) above to capture prey.

Brown Pelicans catch a lot of water along with their prey. They tip their bills downward to drain the water before swallowing the fish. A Brown Pelican's gular pouch can hold up to three gallons of water, three times the bird's total weight. They also use their pouch to carry food to their young.

If this bird looks a little prehistoric, it is because the basic features of all pelicans have changed very little in the last thirty to forty million years. Brown Pelicans incubate their eggs with their webbed feet. Their feet are full of blood vessels that transfer heat to the eggs. Their webbed feet also help make them excellent swimmers.

Pelicans also fly low over the water, taking advantage of slope lift and light upward breezes reflected from the tops of waves.

American Robin

Measurements (Both Sexes)

Length: 7.9–11.0 in. (20–28 cm)

Weight: 2.7–3.0 oz. (77–85 g)

Wingspan: 12.2–15.8 in. (31–40 cm)

Common and widespread all over the continental United States year-round. Sometimes winter in Florida.

Member of the thrush family. Used to be called the American Thrush. Declared a songbird and so was no longer a game bird.

EARLY BIRDS

Why are American Robins so good at catching worms?

American Robins hunt by making short runs or hops, but then they stand entirely still and erect when they detect an earthworm. The American Robin cocks its head to look and listen. Then it grabs the worm with its bill.

Each eye can work independently, so when American Robins cock their heads, they're turning one eye to look more closely at the soil.

Play a tug-of-war game with a friend. One of you is the robin, and the other the worm.

ALMOST FIVE YARDS OF WORMS PUT END TO END

An American Robin may eat up to 14 feet of earthworms in one day!

THOSE WORMS ARE USED TO MAKE BABY FORMULA

Regurgitated worms are superfood for baby robins. Adults actually prefer eating berries.

Ways to help robins find worms

Water the lawn early in the morning to bring worms closer to the surface.

Leave fallen leaves intact for robins to forage and search through. The damp soil under the leaves is an excellent habitat for worms.

Barn Owl

Measurements (Both Sexes)

Length: 12.6–15.8 in. (32–40 cm)

Weight: 14.1–24.7 oz. (400–700 g)

Wingspan: 39.4–49.2 in. (100–125 cm)

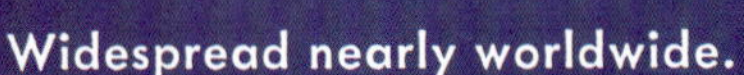

Widespread nearly worldwide.

Habitat: Open country, groves, farms, barns, towns, cliffs, and marshes.

Extreme weather events such as powerful storms, long winter freezes, and increased heat caused by climate change can endanger all owls. Barn Owls are especially vulnerable to freezes becausee they do not store fat In their bodies.

SILENT SWOOPERS

How do owls manage to be so quiet?

Barn Owls are known for their ability to fly silently, making them excellent hunters. They have soft, velvety feathers that reduce noise during flight. Small fibers covering the feathers absorb sound.

Owls also have a unique wing shape designed for quiet flight. Their broad, rounded wings allow them to fly slowly and maintain control.

In addition, they fly close to the ground, minimizing the distance between their wings and the ground. This reduces the amount of air disturbance and noise made during flight. Barn Owls also use updrafts and other air currents to glide silently over their prey.

The Barn Owl has a very engaging face as the eyes and beak are entirely encircled by a heart-shaped ruff of white feathers rimmed with tan feathers. The feathers surrounding its face give it very sensitive hearing. Its heart-shaped face collects sound.

The color of an Owl's eyes tells a story.

Dark brown or black eyes mean that the owl is nocturnal and prefers to hunt at night. This eye color doesn't help them see in the dark, but it helps them blend in with their surroundings. Orange eyes mean that the owl is crepuscular, which means that it is active during low-light periods like dawn and dusk. Yellow eyes mean that the owl is diurnal and likes to hunt during the day. Great Gray Owls have yellow eyes, and their habits are similar to humans—active during the day and sleeping at night.

Barn Owls have a unique ear design that makes them great hunters in the dark. Their ears are not in the same place on their head—one is slightly higher than the other. The left ear captures sound from below, while the right ear listens for sounds coming from above.

Northern Mockingbird

Measurements (Both Sexes)
Length: 8.3–10.2 in. (21–26 cm)
Weight: 1.6–2.0 oz. (45–58 g)
Wingspan: 12.2–13.8 in. (31–35 cm)

Common places to find Northern Mockingbirds include parkland, cultivated land, suburban areas, and in second-growth habitat at low elevations. Although most mockingbirds are not yet in danger from climate change, some living in deserts are vulnerable to increasing heat and drier conditions.

THE GREAT MIMICS

What kinds of sounds can Mockingbirds make?

A Northern Mockingbird may be in a tree at the edge of a yard. When a dog barks, it might respond with a chirp that sounds like a bark. Then, when a siren passes, the Northern Mockingbird might imitate the sound by wailing. If another bird sings, the mockingbird can also mimic its song.

These talkative birds can imitate many sounds, including the chirps of thirty-five different bird species. They can learn over 200 different songs throughout their lifetime. Additionally, they can mimic the sounds created by insects and amphibians, as well as mechanical sounds.

Most species of birds have a range of calls and songs. Often, males use them to attract females and defend their territories. Calls are shorter and simpler and are used by both sexes to sound an alarm, beg for food, or stay in contact with other birds.

While some city dwellers prefer a quiet environment for restful sleep at night, the nocturnal singing of mockingbirds may keep them up. Mockingbirds tend to sing at night as they face less competition from other bird species and city sounds. Mockingbirds have complex songs they use to attract mates and defend territories.

Common Loon

Measurements (Both Sexes)
Length: 26.0–35.8 in. (66–91 cm)
Weight: 88.2–215.2 oz. (2,500–6,100 g)
Wingspan: 40.9–51.6 in. (104–131 cm)

Common and widespread.

Habitat: Clear lakes with coves and islands with plenty of small fish.

THE NORTH'S WILDERNESS SONG

Can Loons really yodel?

The loon can dive deep, up to 180 feet, and remain underwater for 15 minutes! However, its feet are so far back on its body that it cannot walk on land. This makes it difficult for the bird to move around when it needs to sit on its nest.

To gain enough speed for liftoff, loons must flap their wings and run across the top of the water, requiring a distance from 30 yards up to a quarter mile, depending on the wind.

The Common Loon's haunting and beautiful cry embodies the untamed and pristine beauty of the northern wilderness. It serves as a powerful symbol of the vast and unspoiled landscapes that define the region, inspiring nature enthusiasts and conservationists alike.

Loons are birds that make different sounds to communicate with each other. They have four types of calls that they use.

The wail is the most common call that they make, and it helps them find their family or mate.

The hoot is a soft and short call to talk to their family.

The yodel is a call that only male Common Loons make when they feel scared or threatened.

The tremolo is a crazy laugh-like call loons use when they feel scared or threatened. So next time you see Common Loons, remember to keep your distance so they can communicate without feeling scared!

Common Loons are not ducks. Their legs are placed far back on their bodies, which means they cannot easily walk on land. Unlike ducks, they have adapted to living entirely on water.

SHAPE SEEING

When I draw, I like to find shapes within shapes. It's like looking at a puzzle. For example, if I draw the full moon and cut out its shape from light paper and put it on a dark background, it looks more like the moon to me than a pencil outline because its shape has volume. This helps me understand how shapes can help make a picture. I also think about drawing in layers, like making a layer cake. First, I look at the whole shape, then I look for smaller shapes within that shape, like the bird's bill, eyes, wing, and tail.

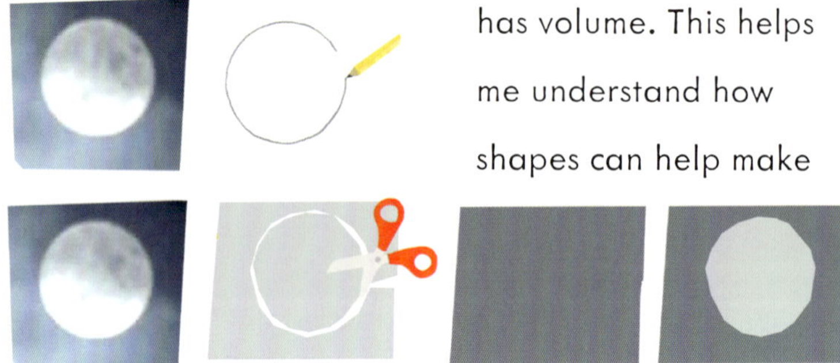

Finally, I think about the colors as shapes within shapes and draw those. It's like putting together a puzzle! Oh, the top layer is like the cake's icing; the other layers are below it.

Cut out shapes and arrange them. Play around with swapping the layers.

AUTHOR'S NOTE

My grandmother read *The Tale of Peter Rabbit* to me when I was young. I later learned that Beatrix Potter created the story as an illustrated letter to comfort a sick child. This inspired me to send daily text messages with pictures of a bird with a heart to my friend Therese, who was seriously ill. I added hearts and bold colors to the artwork to lift her spirits. Thankfully, she is now fully recovered, and I hope these pictures have helped. This book contains some of those pictures.

The art and text in this book are not meant to provide an exhaustive study of bird species. Instead, I would like my reader to slow down, observe, and appreciate the wonders of nature, and engage with the natural world. I invite you to be an active participant in this journey, and I hope you will gain a fresh new look at our world. And if you know someone who is not feeling well, make them a picture, send them a note, or do both. This way, we can really help those who need our love and support.

In creating the illustrations for my book, I drew from a wide variety of references and experiences gathered over a lifetime of observation. I am also thankful to amateur photographers who share their backyard snapshots, as their contributions deepen my understanding of the subjects I portray.

OFF YOU GO!

Online Resources for Bird Information

Cornell Lab of Ornithology—Merlin Bird ID

https://merlin.allaboutbirds.org/

Merlin is a user-friendly app and website created by the Cornell Lab of Ornithology that helps you identify birds based on their features and sounds. You can answer a few simple questions about the bird you saw—like its color, size, and location—and Merlin will suggest possible matches. It's a fun tool to help you learn about different bird species!

eBird

https://ebird.org/home

eBird is an online platform that allows bird watchers to record their sightings and share information about bird populations around the world. You can explore maps, browse regular updates about bird activity, and even see which birds are reported most often in your area. This site can help you learn about local birds and their habits.

Birds of the World

https://birdsoftheworld.org

This is a comprehensive resource where you can find detailed information about various bird species, including their habitats, behaviors, and conservation status. The website features articles, images, and audio recordings of birds which can greatly enhance your understanding of different types of birds.

National Audubon Society

https://www.audubon.org/

The National Audubon Society is dedicated to protecting birds and their habitats. Their website provides a wealth of information about bird conservation, bird-watching tips, and educational resources for kids. You can also find bird guides and ways to get involved in local bird conservation efforts.

All About Birds

https://www.allaboutbirds.org/

This site, run by the Cornell Lab of Ornithology, offers a vast collection of articles, videos, and interactive tools about birds. It's perfect for kids to explore different bird species, learn calls and songs, and gain a deeper understanding of how to protect birds and their environments.

Research Local Nature Centers Search for nearby nature centers and wildlife refuges.

Contact Local Audubon Chapters Reach out for recommendations on bird-watching events and locations.

Explore Parks and Reserves Visit local or national parks with bird-watching areas and visitor centers.

Create Your Own Bird-Watching Group Form a group with friends to observe birds in local parks.

Don't overlook the resources available at public libraries and bookshops. They can be invaluable for research, leisure reading, and discovering new topics of interest.

INDEX